© BIZZJOY PRESS (2020)

Quick Reference CPD & Training Log

Date	Type (Book etc)	Title	By (Author, trainer etc)	Total Cost	CPD Cert (✓)	CPD Hrs

Quick Reference CPD & Training Log

Date	Type (Book etc)	Title	By (Author, trainer etc)	Total Cost	CPD Cert (✓)	CPD Hrs

Notes

CPD / Training Record

Date	Title	Author / Trainer etc	
		Company (if applicable)	

Reason(s) for CPD	Planned ✓	Unplanned ✓

Reflection / Learning

Star Rating (Circle) 　　　　　* * * * *

Further CPD and Research Recommended

Type (Book, course, website, workshop etc)	Title

Personal or Professional Impact

Breakdown costs of CPD		Total	
Purchase Cost			
Travel			
Accommodation			
Incidentals			

CPD / Training Record

Date	Title	Author / Trainer etc	
		Company (if applicable)	

Reason(s) for CPD	Planned ✓	Unplanned ✓

Reflection / Learning

Star Rating (Circle)   *   *   *   *   *

Further CPD and Research Recommended	
Type (Book, course, website, workshop etc)	**Title**

Personal or Professional Impact

Breakdown costs of CPD		Total	
Purchase Cost			
Travel			
Accommodation			
Incidentals			

CPD / Training Record

Date	Title	Author / Trainer etc	
		Company (if applicable)	

Reason(s) for CPD	Planned ✓	Unplanned ✓

Reflection / Learning

Star Rating (Circle)	* * * * *

Further CPD and Research Recommended

Type (Book, course, website, workshop etc)	Title

Personal or Professional Impact

Breakdown costs of CPD		Total	
Purchase Cost			
Travel			
Accommodation			
Incidentals			

CPD / Training Record

Date	Title	Author / Trainer etc	
		Company (if applicable)	

Reason(s) for CPD	Planned ✓	Unplanned ✓

Reflection / Learning

Star Rating (Circle)   *   *   *   *   *

Further CPD and Research Recommended	
Type (Book, course, website, workshop etc)	**Title**

Personal or Professional Impact

Breakdown costs of CPD		Total	
Purchase Cost			
Travel			
Accommodation			
Incidentals			

CPD / Training Record

Date	Title	Author / Trainer etc	
		Company (if applicable)	

Reason(s) for CPD	Planned ✓	Unplanned ✓

Reflection / Learning

Star Rating (Circle)	* * * * *

Further CPD and Research Recommended

Type (Book, course, website, workshop etc)	Title

Personal or Professional Impact

Breakdown costs of CPD	**Total**
Purchase Cost	
Travel	
Accommodation	
Incidentals	

CPD / Training Record

Date	Title	Author / Trainer etc	
		Company (if applicable)	

Reason(s) for CPD	Planned ✓	Unplanned ✓

Reflection / Learning

Star Rating (Circle)   * * * * *

Further CPD and Research Recommended

Type (Book, course, website, workshop etc)	Title

Personal or Professional Impact

Breakdown costs of CPD		Total	
Purchase Cost			
Travel			
Accommodation			
Incidentals			

CPD / Training Record

Date	Title	Author / Trainer etc	
		Company (if applicable)	

Reason(s) for CPD	Planned ✓	Unplanned ✓

Reflection / Learning

Star Rating (Circle) 　　　　　　　　＊　＊　＊　＊　＊

Further CPD and Research Recommended	
Type (Book, course, website, workshop etc)	**Title**

Personal or Professional Impact

Breakdown costs of CPD		Total	
Purchase Cost			
Travel			
Accommodation			
Incidentals			

CPD / Training Record

Date	Title	Author / Trainer etc	
		Company (if applicable)	

Reason(s) for CPD	Planned ✓	Unplanned ✓

Reflection / Learning

Star Rating (Circle) 　　　　　* * * * *

Further CPD and Research Recommended	
Type (Book, course, website, workshop etc)	**Title**

Personal or Professional Impact

Breakdown costs of CPD	Total	
Purchase Cost		
Travel		
Accommodation		
Incidentals		

CPD / Training Record

Date	Title	Author / Trainer etc	
		Company (if applicable)	

Reason(s) for CPD	Planned ✓	Unplanned ✓

Reflection / Learning

Star Rating (Circle) — * * * * *

Further CPD and Research Recommended

Type (Book, course, website, workshop etc)	Title

Personal or Professional Impact

Breakdown costs of CPD		Total	
Purchase Cost			
Travel			
Accommodation			
Incidentals			

CPD / Training Record

Date	Title	Author / Trainer etc	
		Company (if applicable)	

	Planned ✓	Unplanned ✓
Reason(s) for CPD		

Reflection / Learning

Star Rating (Circle)	* * * * *

Further CPD and Research Recommended

Type (Book, course, website, workshop etc)	Title

Personal or Professional Impact

Breakdown costs of CPD	Total	
Purchase Cost		
Travel		
Accommodation		
Incidentals		

CPD / Training Record

Date	Title	Author / Trainer etc	
		Company (if applicable)	

Reason(s) for CPD	Planned ✓	Unplanned ✓

Reflection / Learning

Star Rating (Circle)   * * * * *

Further CPD and Research Recommended	
Type (Book, course, website, workshop etc)	**Title**

Personal or Professional Impact

Breakdown costs of CPD		Total	
Purchase Cost			
Travel			
Accommodation			
Incidentals			

CPD / Training Record

Date	Title	Author / Trainer etc	
		Company (if applicable)	

	Planned ✓	Unplanned ✓
Reason(s) for CPD		

Reflection / Learning

Star Rating (Circle)   * * * * *

Further CPD and Research Recommended	
Type (Book, course, website, workshop etc)	**Title**

Personal or Professional Impact

Breakdown costs of CPD		Total	
Purchase Cost			
Travel			
Accommodation			
Incidentals			

CPD / Training Record

Date	Title	Author / Trainer etc	
		Company (if applicable)	

Reason(s) for CPD	Planned ✓	Unplanned ✓

Reflection / Learning

Star Rating (Circle)	✶ ✶ ✶ ✶ ✶

Further CPD and Research Recommended	
Type (Book, course, website, workshop etc)	**Title**

Personal or Professional Impact

Breakdown costs of CPD	Total
Purchase Cost	
Travel	
Accommodation	
Incidentals	

CPD / Training Record				
Date	**Title**	**Author / Trainer etc**		
		Company (if applicable)		
Reason(s) for CPD			Planned ✓	Unplanned ✓

Reflection / Learning

Star Rating (Circle)	* * * * *

Further CPD and Research Recommended	
Type (Book, course, website, workshop etc)	**Title**

Personal or Professional Impact

_____
_____
_____
_____
_____
_____
_____
_____
_____
_____

Breakdown costs of CPD		Total	
Purchase Cost			
Travel			
Accommodation			
Incidentals			

CPD / Training Record

Date	Title	Author / Trainer etc	
		Company (if applicable)	

Reason(s) for CPD	Planned ✓	Unplanned ✓

Reflection / Learning

Star Rating (Circle)   * * * * *

Further CPD and Research Recommended

Type (Book, course, website, workshop etc)	Title

Personal or Professional Impact

Breakdown costs of CPD		Total	
Purchase Cost			
Travel			
Accommodation			
Incidentals			

	CPD / Training Record			
Date	**Title**	**Author / Trainer etc**		
		Company (if applicable)		
	Reason(s) for CPD		Planned ✓	Unplanned ✓

Reflection / Learning

Star Rating (Circle)	* * * * *

Further CPD and Research Recommended	
Type (Book, course, website, workshop etc)	**Title**

Personal or Professional Impact

Breakdown costs of CPD		Total	
Purchase Cost			
Travel			
Accommodation			
Incidentals			

CPD / Training Record

Date	Title	Author / Trainer etc	
		Company (if applicable)	

Reason(s) for CPD	Planned ✓	Unplanned ✓

Reflection / Learning

Star Rating (Circle)   * * * * *

Further CPD and Research Recommended	
Type (Book, course, website, workshop etc)	**Title**

Personal or Professional Impact

Breakdown costs of CPD		Total	
Purchase Cost			
Travel			
Accommodation			
Incidentals			

CPD / Training Record

Date	Title	Author / Trainer etc	
		Company (if applicable)	

Reason(s) for CPD	Planned ✓	Unplanned ✓

Reflection / Learning

Star Rating (Circle)	* * * * *

Further CPD and Research Recommended	
Type (Book, course, website, workshop etc)	**Title**

Personal or Professional Impact

Breakdown costs of CPD		Total	
Purchase Cost			
Travel			
Accommodation			
Incidentals			

CPD / Training Record

Date	Title	Author / Trainer etc	
		Company (if applicable)	

Reason(s) for CPD	Planned ✓	Unplanned ✓

Reflection / Learning

Star Rating (Circle)   ✱ ✱ ✱ ✱ ✱

Further CPD and Research Recommended	
Type (Book, course, website, workshop etc)	**Title**

Personal or Professional Impact

Breakdown costs of CPD		Total	
Purchase Cost			
Travel			
Accommodation			
Incidentals			

CPD / Training Record

Date	Title	Author / Trainer etc	
		Company (if applicable)	

Reason(s) for CPD	Planned ✓	Unplanned ✓

Reflection / Learning

Star Rating (Circle)   * * * * *

Further CPD and Research Recommended	
Type (Book, course, website, workshop etc)	**Title**

Personal or Professional Impact

Breakdown costs of CPD		Total	
Purchase Cost			
Travel			
Accommodation			
Incidentals			

CPD / Training Record

Date	Title	Author / Trainer etc	
		Company (if applicable)	

Reason(s) for CPD	Planned ✓	Unplanned ✓

Reflection / Learning

Star Rating (Circle) 　　　　　＊　＊　＊　＊　＊

Further CPD and Research Recommended	
Type (Book, course, website, workshop etc)	**Title**

Personal or Professional Impact

Breakdown costs of CPD		Total	
Purchase Cost			
Travel			
Accommodation			
Incidentals			

CPD / Training Record

Date	Title	Author / Trainer etc	
		Company (if applicable)	

Reason(s) for CPD	Planned ✓	Unplanned ✓

Reflection / Learning

Star Rating (Circle)   * * * * *

Further CPD and Research Recommended	
Type (Book, course, website, workshop etc)	**Title**

Personal or Professional Impact

Breakdown costs of CPD	Total	
Purchase Cost		
Travel		
Accommodation		
Incidentals		

CPD / Training Record

Date	Title	Author / Trainer etc	
		Company (if applicable)	

Reason(s) for CPD	Planned ✓	Unplanned ✓

Reflection / Learning

Star Rating (Circle) ✶ ✶ ✶ ✶ ✶

Further CPD and Research Recommended	
Type (Book, course, website, workshop etc)	**Title**

Personal or Professional Impact

Breakdown costs of CPD		Total	
Purchase Cost			
Travel			
Accommodation			
Incidentals			

CPD / Training Record

Date	Title	Author / Trainer etc	
		Company (if applicable)	

Reason(s) for CPD	Planned ✓	Unplanned ✓

Reflection / Learning

Star Rating (Circle)	* * * * *

Further CPD and Research Recommended	
Type (Book, course, website, workshop etc)	**Title**

Personal or Professional Impact

Breakdown costs of CPD		Total	
Purchase Cost			
Travel			
Accommodation			
Incidentals			

CPD / Training Record

Date	Title	Author / Trainer etc	
		Company (if applicable)	

Reason(s) for CPD	Planned ✓	Unplanned ✓

Reflection / Learning

Star Rating (Circle)　　　　　* * * * *

Further CPD and Research Recommended	
Type (Book, course, website, workshop etc)	**Title**

Personal or Professional Impact

Breakdown costs of CPD		Total	
Purchase Cost			
Travel			
Accommodation			
Incidentals			

CPD / Training Record

Date	Title	Author / Trainer etc	
		Company (if applicable)	

Reason(s) for CPD	Planned ✓	Unplanned ✓

Reflection / Learning

Star Rating (Circle)	* * * * *

Further CPD and Research Recommended

Type (Book, course, website, workshop etc)	Title

Personal or Professional Impact

Breakdown costs of CPD		Total	
Purchase Cost			
Travel			
Accommodation			
Incidentals			

CPD / Training Record

Date	Title	Author / Trainer etc	
		Company (if applicable)	

Reason(s) for CPD	Planned ✓	Unplanned ✓

Reflection / Learning

Star Rating (Circle)   ✱ ✱ ✱ ✱ ✱

Further CPD and Research Recommended

Type (Book, course, website, workshop etc)	Title

Personal or Professional Impact

Breakdown costs of CPD		Total	
Purchase Cost			
Travel			
Accommodation			
Incidentals			

CPD / Training Record

Date	Title	Author / Trainer etc	
		Company (if applicable)	

Reason(s) for CPD	Planned ✓	Unplanned ✓

Reflection / Learning

Star Rating (Circle)	* * * * *

Further CPD and Research Recommended

Type (Book, course, website, workshop etc)	Title

Personal or Professional Impact

Breakdown costs of CPD		Total	
Purchase Cost			
Travel			
Accommodation			
Incidentals			

CPD / Training Record

Date	Title	Author / Trainer etc	
		Company (if applicable)	

Reason(s) for CPD	Planned ✓	Unplanned ✓

Reflection / Learning

Star Rating (Circle)   * * * * *

Further CPD and Research Recommended	
Type (Book, course, website, workshop etc)	**Title**

Personal or Professional Impact

Breakdown costs of CPD	Total	
Purchase Cost		
Travel		
Accommodation		
Incidentals		

CPD / Training Record

Date	Title	Author / Trainer etc	
		Company (if applicable)	

Reason(s) for CPD	Planned ✓	Unplanned ✓

Reflection / Learning

Star Rating (Circle)	* * * * *

Further CPD and Research Recommended

Type (Book, course, website, workshop etc)	Title

Personal or Professional Impact

Breakdown costs of CPD		Total	
Purchase Cost			
Travel			
Accommodation			
Incidentals			

CPD / Training Record

Date	Title	Author / Trainer etc	
		Company (if applicable)	

Reason(s) for CPD	Planned ✓	Unplanned ✓

Reflection / Learning

Star Rating (Circle)	* * * * *

Further CPD and Research Recommended	
Type (Book, course, website, workshop etc)	**Title**

Personal or Professional Impact

Breakdown costs of CPD		Total	
Purchase Cost			
Travel			
Accommodation			
Incidentals			

CPD / Training Record

Date	Title	Author / Trainer etc	
		Company (if applicable)	

Reason(s) for CPD	Planned ✓	Unplanned ✓

Reflection / Learning

Star Rating (Circle)   * * * * *

Further CPD and Research Recommended	
Type (Book, course, website, workshop etc)	**Title**

Personal or Professional Impact

Breakdown costs of CPD		Total	
Purchase Cost			
Travel			
Accommodation			
Incidentals			

CPD / Training Record

Date	Title	Author / Trainer etc	
		Company (if applicable)	

Reason(s) for CPD	Planned ✓	Unplanned ✓

Reflection / Learning

Star Rating (Circle) * * * * *

Further CPD and Research Recommended

Type (Book, course, website, workshop etc)	Title

Personal or Professional Impact

Breakdown costs of CPD	Total	
Purchase Cost		
Travel		
Accommodation		
Incidentals		

CPD / Training Record

Date	Title	Author / Trainer etc	
		Company (if applicable)	

Reason(s) for CPD	Planned ✓	Unplanned ✓

Reflection / Learning

Star Rating (Circle) * * * * *

Further CPD and Research Recommended	
Type (Book, course, website, workshop etc)	**Title**

Personal or Professional Impact

Breakdown costs of CPD	Total	
Purchase Cost		
Travel		
Accommodation		
Incidentals		

CPD / Training Record

Date	Title	Author / Trainer etc	
		Company (if applicable)	

Reason(s) for CPD	Planned ✓	Unplanned ✓

Reflection / Learning

Star Rating (Circle)   ✶ ✶ ✶ ✶ ✶

Further CPD and Research Recommended

Type (Book, course, website, workshop etc)	Title

Personal or Professional Impact

Breakdown costs of CPD | Total |

Purchase Cost	
Travel	
Accommodation	
Incidentals	

CPD / Training Record

Date	Title	Author / Trainer etc	
		Company (if applicable)	

Reason(s) for CPD	Planned ✓	Unplanned ✓

Reflection / Learning

Star Rating (Circle) — * * * * *

Further CPD and Research Recommended

Type (Book, course, website, workshop etc)	Title

Personal or Professional Impact

Breakdown costs of CPD		Total	
Purchase Cost			
Travel			
Accommodation			
Incidentals			

CPD / Training Record

Date	Title	Author / Trainer etc	
		Company (if applicable)	

Reason(s) for CPD	Planned ✓	Unplanned ✓

Reflection / Learning

Star Rating (Circle)	* * * * *

Further CPD and Research Recommended

Type (Book, course, website, workshop etc)	Title

Personal or Professional Impact

Breakdown costs of CPD		Total	
Purchase Cost			
Travel			
Accommodation			
Incidentals			

CPD / Training Record

Date	Title	Author / Trainer etc	
		Company (if applicable)	

Reason(s) for CPD	Planned ✓	Unplanned ✓

Reflection / Learning

Star Rating (Circle)   *   *   *   *   *

Further CPD and Research Recommended

Type (Book, course, website, workshop etc)	Title

Personal or Professional Impact

Breakdown costs of CPD | Total |

Purchase Cost	
Travel	
Accommodation	
Incidentals	

CPD / Training Record

Date	Title	Author / Trainer etc	
		Company (if applicable)	

Reason(s) for CPD	Planned ✓	Unplanned ✓

Reflection / Learning

Star Rating (Circle)	* * * * *

Further CPD and Research Recommended	
Type (Book, course, website, workshop etc)	**Title**

Personal or Professional Impact

Breakdown costs of CPD		Total	
Purchase Cost			
Travel			
Accommodation			
Incidentals			

CPD / Training Record

Date	Title	Author / Trainer etc	
		Company (if applicable)	

Reason(s) for CPD	Planned ✓	Unplanned ✓

Reflection / Learning

Star Rating (Circle)	* * * * *

Further CPD and Research Recommended

Type (Book, course, website, workshop etc)	Title

Personal or Professional Impact

Breakdown costs of CPD		Total	
Purchase Cost			
Travel			
Accommodation			
Incidentals			

CPD / Training Record

Date	Title	Author / Trainer etc	
		Company (if applicable)	

Reason(s) for CPD	Planned ✓	Unplanned ✓

Reflection / Learning

Star Rating (Circle)	* * * * *

Further CPD and Research Recommended	
Type (Book, course, website, workshop etc)	**Title**

Personal or Professional Impact

Breakdown costs of CPD		Total	
Purchase Cost			
Travel			
Accommodation			
Incidentals			

CPD / Training Record

Date	Title	Author / Trainer etc	
		Company (if applicable)	

Reason(s) for CPD	Planned ✓	Unplanned ✓

Reflection / Learning

Star Rating (Circle)   * * * * *

Further CPD and Research Recommended	
Type (Book, course, website, workshop etc)	**Title**

Personal or Professional Impact

Breakdown costs of CPD	Total	
Purchase Cost		
Travel		
Accommodation		
Incidentals		

CPD / Training Record

Date	Title	Author / Trainer etc		
		Company (if applicable)		

Reason(s) for CPD	Planned ✓	Unplanned ✓

Reflection / Learning

Star Rating (Circle)	* * * * *

Further CPD and Research Recommended	
Type (Book, course, website, workshop etc)	**Title**

Personal or Professional Impact

Breakdown costs of CPD	Total	
Purchase Cost		
Travel		
Accommodation		
Incidentals		

CPD / Training Record

Date	Title	Author / Trainer etc	
		Company (if applicable)	

Reason(s) for CPD	Planned ✓	Unplanned ✓

Reflection / Learning

Star Rating (Circle)   * * * * *

Further CPD and Research Recommended	
Type (Book, course, website, workshop etc)	**Title**

Personal or Professional Impact

Breakdown costs of CPD	Total	
Purchase Cost		
Travel		
Accommodation		
Incidentals		

CPD / Training Record

Date	Title	Author / Trainer etc	
		Company (if applicable)	

Reason(s) for CPD	Planned ✓	Unplanned ✓

Reflection / Learning

Star Rating (Circle)   * * * * *

Further CPD and Research Recommended	
Type (Book, course, website, workshop etc)	**Title**

Personal or Professional Impact

Breakdown costs of CPD		Total	
Purchase Cost			
Travel			
Accommodation			
Incidentals			

CPD / Training Record

Date	Title	Author / Trainer etc	
		Company (if applicable)	

Reason(s) for CPD	Planned ✓	Unplanned ✓

Reflection / Learning

Star Rating (Circle)   * * * * *

Further CPD and Research Recommended	
Type (Book, course, website, workshop etc)	**Title**

Personal or Professional Impact

Breakdown costs of CPD		Total	
Purchase Cost			
Travel			
Accommodation			
Incidentals			

CPD / Training Record

Date	Title	Author / Trainer etc		
		Company (if applicable)		

Reason(s) for CPD	Planned ✓	Unplanned ✓

Reflection / Learning

Star Rating (Circle)   * * * * *

Further CPD and Research Recommended	
Type (Book, course, website, workshop etc)	**Title**

Personal or Professional Impact

Breakdown costs of CPD		Total	
Purchase Cost			
Travel			
Accommodation			
Incidentals			

CPD / Training Record

Date	Title	Author / Trainer etc	
		Company (if applicable)	

Reason(s) for CPD	Planned ✓	Unplanned ✓

Reflection / Learning

Star Rating (Circle)	* * * * *

Further CPD and Research Recommended

Type (Book, course, website, workshop etc)	Title

Personal or Professional Impact

Breakdown costs of CPD	Total	
Purchase Cost		
Travel		
Accommodation		
Incidentals		

CPD / Training Record

Date	Title	Author / Trainer etc	
		Company (if applicable)	

Reason(s) for CPD	Planned ✓	Unplanned ✓

Reflection / Learning

Star Rating (Circle)   * * * * *

Further CPD and Research Recommended	
Type (Book, course, website, workshop etc)	**Title**

Personal or Professional Impact

Breakdown costs of CPD	Total	
Purchase Cost		
Travel		
Accommodation		
Incidentals		

CPD / Training Record

Date	Title	Author / Trainer etc	
		Company (if applicable)	

Reason(s) for CPD	Planned ✓	Unplanned ✓

Reflection / Learning

Star Rating (Circle)   * * * * *

Further CPD and Research Recommended	
Type (Book, course, website, workshop etc)	**Title**

Personal or Professional Impact

Breakdown costs of CPD	Total	
Purchase Cost		
Travel		
Accommodation		
Incidentals		

Notes

Printed in Great Britain
by Amazon